Passport to World Communities

Carol Aronin
Social Studies Consultant
Syosset, New York

Michael A. Colucci
Social Studies Consultant
Historian
Valley Cottage, New York

Editorial Offices: Glenview, Illinois • Parsippany, New Jersey • New York, New York
Sales Offices: Parsippany, New Jersey • Duluth, Georgia • Glenview, Illinois •
Coppell, Texas • Ontario, California • Mesa, Arizona

www.sfsocialstudies.com

ISBN: 0-328-03897-0

11 V042 11 10 09

Contents

Unit 3

Welcome to Brazil!

Unit 4

Welcome to Spain!

Unit 5

Unit 6

Document-Based Questions

Documents help readers learn new things. Maps, pictures, charts, and stories from history are different kinds of documents. Documents that were written by people who were at an event and saw it or who lived at that time are called primary sources. Look at each document and answer the question that follows it. Use the information from each document, your answers to the Document-Based Questions, and your knowledge of social studies to write a paragraph that answers the Tying It All Together question.

Document 1: Historical Narrative

June 1942
Hoed the raspberry & [and] strawberry rows; peas, 2 rows, 35 melon hills . . . yesterday. Today hoed corn, 5 rows, 4 rows potatoes . . . beets, lettuce, [and so on], a big hard job. Have to weed each row by hand; mostly grass in the rows.

June 1944
This week I have put in [planted] potatoes, corn, radishes, peas & beans & hoed the garden, cut 30 large thistles [plants with prickly stalks] today out of . . . [the] alfalfa field.

—Excerpts taken from *All Will Yet Be Well: The Diary of Sarah Gillespie Huftalen, 1873–1952* Edited by Suzanne L. Bunkers

▶ Sarah Gillespie Huftalen began to write in a diary when she was a pioneer girl on a farm in Iowa. She became a teacher and also continued to do farm work. She wrote in a diary for over 70 years.

🔍 **DOCUMENT-BASED QUESTION** *What are three kinds of food that Sarah plants?*

Document 2: Painting

▶ This painting shows peasants harvesting grain in the 1500s.

🔍 **DOCUMENT-BASED QUESTION** *How does the painting show that harvesting grain is hard work?*

Document 3: Map of Australia

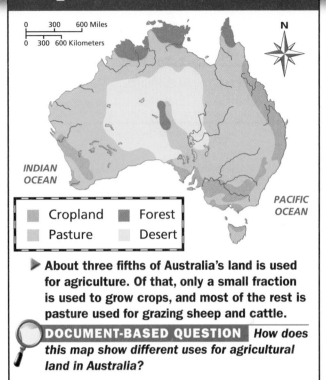

0 300 600 Miles
0 300 600 Kilometers

N

INDIAN OCEAN

PACIFIC OCEAN

Legend:
- Cropland
- Forest
- Pasture
- Desert

▶ About three fifths of Australia's land is used for agriculture. Of that, only a small fraction is used to grow crops, and most of the rest is pasture used for grazing sheep and cattle.

🔍 **DOCUMENT-BASED QUESTION** *How does this map show different uses for agricultural land in Australia?*

Document 4: Photograph

▶ Rice is the major crop of China.

🔍 **DOCUMENT-BASED QUESTION** *What do you notice about how the farmers work in their rice fields?*

🔍 Tying It All Together

Based on the historical narrative, painting, map, and photograph on these pages, describe different ways people use land as a source for food?

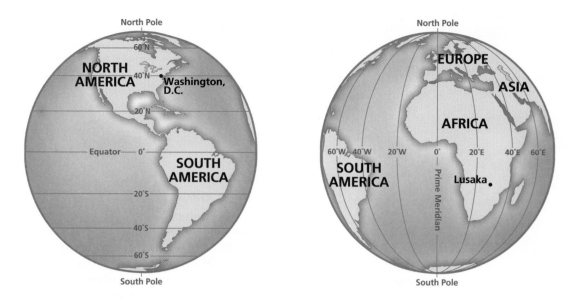

▶ **Latitude and longitude lines can help you locate a place on a map or globe.**

Understand Latitude and Longitude

Latitude and longitude are sets of imaginary lines drawn on a map or globe. These lines are numbered in distances called degrees and can locate places exactly. Latitude lines run east and west around Earth. Their numbers show how far a place is north or south of the latitude line known as the equator, which is numbered 0°.

Longitude lines run north and south between the North and South Poles. Their numbers show how far a place is east or west of the longitude line known as the prime meridian, which is numbered 0°. All meridians are the same length. Lines of latitude and longitude cross, and their numbers at that point are said to locate a place's exact "address."

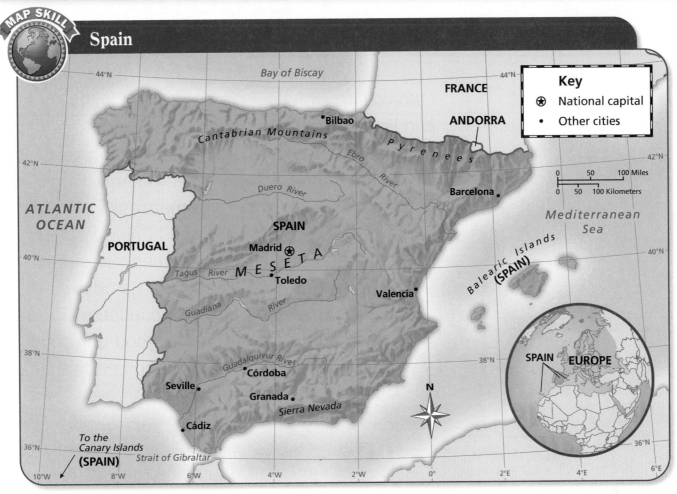

Spain

Key
⊛ National capital
• Other cities

Bay of Biscay
FRANCE
ANDORRA
Bilbao
Cantabrian Mountains
P y r e n e e s
Ebro River
Barcelona
ATLANTIC OCEAN
Duero River
SPAIN
PORTUGAL
Madrid ⊛
M E S E T A
Tagus River
Toledo
Valencia
Guadiana River
Balearic Islands (SPAIN)
Mediterranean Sea
Guadalquivir River
Córdoba
Seville
Granada
Sierra Nevada
Cádiz
To the Canary Islands (SPAIN)
Strait of Gibraltar
N
SPAIN   EUROPE

0   50   100 Miles
0   50   100 Kilometers

44°N 42°N 40°N 38°N 36°N
10°W 8°W 6°W 4°W 2°W 0° 2°E 4°E 6°E

▶ Cádiz is located on the Atlantic coast of Spain. Find the Atlantic coast. Then look along the coast until you find Cádiz.

Directions, Distance, Location, and Scale

Another way to help locate places on a map is by using a compass rose. It points out the cardinal directions of north, south, east, and west, as well as the intermediate, or in-between, directions. Therefore, you can say the location of Granada is south of Madrid.

Adding distance shows a location more exactly. Use a map's scale. Its distance in inches lets you mark distance in miles on Earth. Now you can say Granada is south of Madrid by about 200 miles.

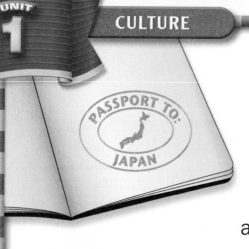

Welcome to Japan!

Konichiwa (koh NEE chee wah)! I'm Yoshi, and I just said "Hello!" in Japanese.

My family lives in an apartment in Tokyo. It is smaller than houses we see on American TV programs. I sleep on a floor mattress called a futon (FOO ton). My family and I enjoy watching television and playing video games. Someday I would like a job designing video games.

I work very hard in school because my family wants me to get into a good university. My classes start at 8:30 A.M. and end at 3:00 P.M. I also attend classes on every other Saturday morning. Two days a week, after regular school is over, I go to a special school called *juku*. Juku helps me get ready for middle and high school.

I like to read Japanese folktales. My favorite is "Momotaro." It is about a boy who, with the help of his animal friends, defeats some ogres, or make-believe giants. Folktales teach me about the ideas and beliefs of my people, which are important to learn too!

▶ **Yoshi lives in Tokyo. It is the largest city in Japan.**

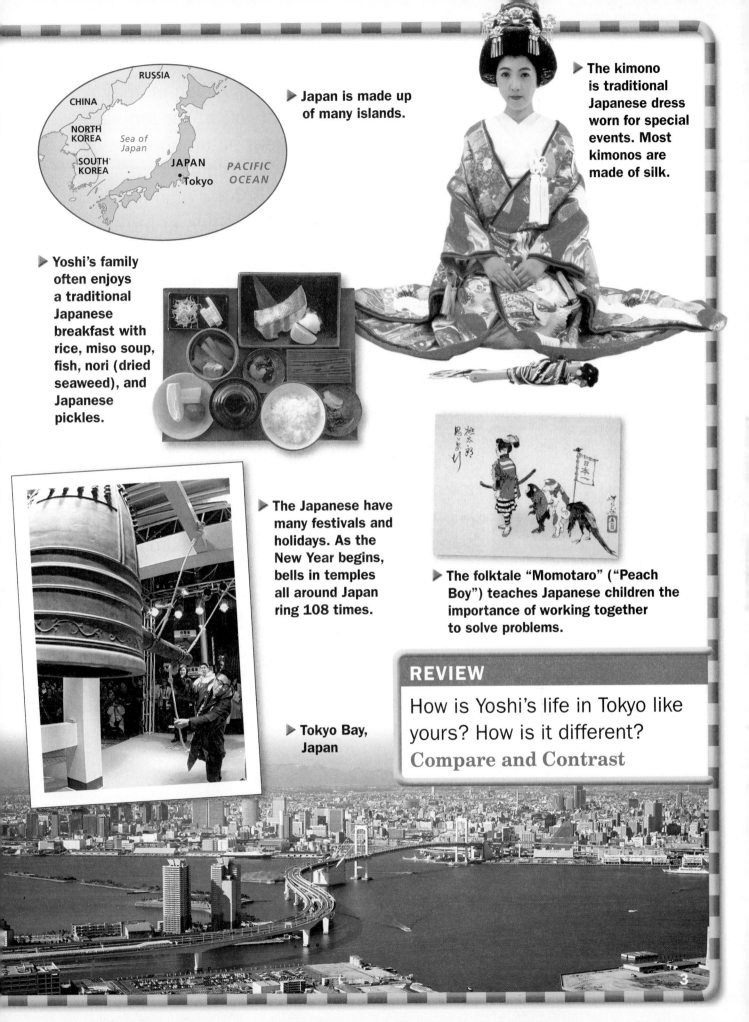

▶ Japan is made up of many islands.

▶ The kimono is traditional Japanese dress worn for special events. Most kimonos are made of silk.

RUSSIA
CHINA
NORTH KOREA
Sea of Japan
SOUTH KOREA
JAPAN
Tokyo
PACIFIC OCEAN

▶ Yoshi's family often enjoys a traditional Japanese breakfast with rice, miso soup, fish, nori (dried seaweed), and Japanese pickles.

▶ The Japanese have many festivals and holidays. As the New Year begins, bells in temples all around Japan ring 108 times.

▶ The folktale "Momotaro" ("Peach Boy") teaches Japanese children the importance of working together to solve problems.

▶ Tokyo Bay, Japan

REVIEW

How is Yoshi's life in Tokyo like yours? How is it different?
Compare and Contrast

3

The Geography of Japan

When many people think of Japan, they think of the busy city of Tokyo. Yet Japan is also a country of great natural beauty. Mountains and hills cover almost three-fourths of the country. But the mountains are not good locations for cities or farms. Japan's biggest cities and best farmland are located on the plains along the coasts.

Japan is located in the Pacific Ocean. It is made up of four large islands and thousands of smaller ones. These islands are off the east coast of Asia, separated by the Sea of Japan from Russia, North and South Korea, and China.

The island of Hokkaido (hoh KY doh) lies farthest north. It is Japan's second largest island, but it has a small population. In winter, people ski in the mountains. In summer, vacationers enjoy the lakes. Hokkaido's green valleys have dairy, potato, and onion farms.

A 34-mile underwater tunnel joins the island of Hokkaido to Japan's largest island, Honshu (HON shyoo). Honshu has Japan's largest population, biggest lake, and tallest mountains. Tokyo is located on Honshu.

▶ Mount Fuji, on the island of Honshu, is the tallest peak in Japan. It is an active volcano.

Japan and Its Neighbors

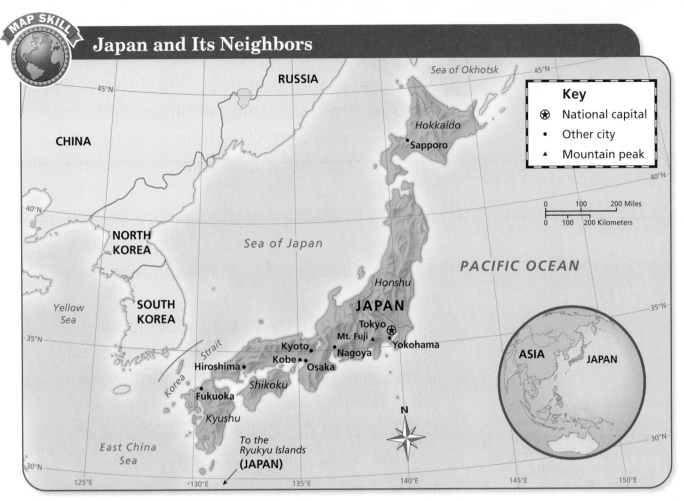

▶ Japan is part of Asia, although it is made up of islands off the mainland.

MAP SKILL Landforms and Water *What large body of water separates the north and west coasts of Japan from the Asian mainland?*

Shikoku (shee KOH kyoo) is the smallest of the four islands. This island is covered with many mountains. Few people live on Shikoku. It is known for vegetable farms and copper mines.

Kyushu (KYOO shoo) is the farthest south of the four big islands. Level strips of farmland have been cut into mountainsides. Kyushu's plains have many cities and factories, and its steep mountains have many volcanoes. Volcanoes and earthquakes have formed much of Japan's geography.

▶ Farmers have turned strips of Kyushu mountainside into productive land.

REVIEW How are the islands of Honshu and Shikoku alike and different?
Compare and Contrast

5

The History of Japan

It is estimated that people first migrated to Japan from the Asian mainland at least 10,000 years ago. Over time, they formed a society, or an organized community with rules and traditions. Contact with China and Korea brought new ideas to this society. People in Japan learned to grow rice in irrigated fields. They began to settle in communities near the rice fields.

As hundreds of years went by, Japan borrowed many ideas. In the 300s, people in Japan learned artistic and metalworking skills from Korea. In the 400s and 500s, they adopted the Chinese writing system.

In the 300s the Yamato Era began. An era is a period of time measured by events, not by exact years. A member of the Yamato family ruled Japan as the first emperor. When this era ended, military leaders took over. The emperor was given less power.

▶ According to Japanese legend, Jimmu Tenno was the first Japanese emperor. He probably was a real ruler, but not until hundreds of years later.

▶ Edo became Japan's capital in the 1600s when Himeji castle was built. Edo is now called Tokyo.

6

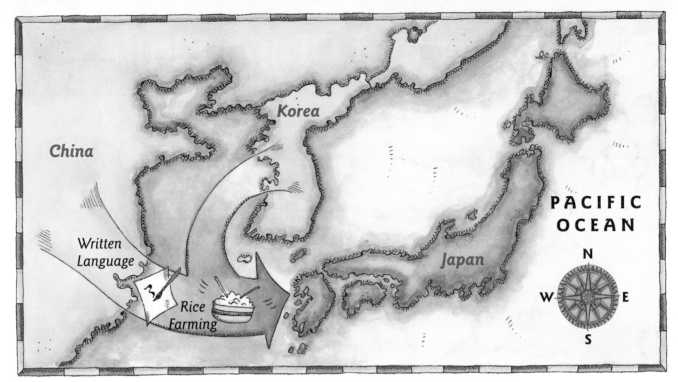

▶ Japan has often accepted ideas from other countries around the world.

🔍 **DOCUMENT-BASED QUESTION** *Why do you think China and Korea had such a strong influence on Japan in its early history?*

To protect Japan, military leaders closed the country off from the outside world for two centuries. In 1854 the United States encouraged Japan to open its ports for trade with other countries. Then in 1868, an emperor took power back from the military leaders.

Japan became very strong. It fought against the United States, England, and other countries in World War II. Bombs destroyed two of Japan's cities. Japan was defeated, but with the help of the United States, Japan grew strong again. Now Japan enjoys peace and democracy.

▶ Japan's contributions to the art world include kabuki, a Japanese form of theater.

REVIEW What happened after Japanese people learned to grow rice in irrigated fields? **Sequence**

7

Use a Time Line

What? A **time line** shows when events occurred. A time line can be a way of counting years. One system of counting is based on the year that Jesus Christ was born. Many people believe that was about 2,000 years ago. Dates before the birth of Jesus Christ are labeled B.C., or "before Christ" on the time line. In B.C., you count backwards from zero on the time line. As you count backwards in the B.C. section of the time line, the numbers get larger. Dates after the birth of Christ are A.D., or *anno Domini*, which means "in the year of our Lord" in Latin. These dates are counted forward from zero.

In both B.C. and A.D., calendar time can be measured in decades (10 years), centuries (100 years), or millennia (1,000 years). Eras may cover a short or long span of time.

Events in the History of Japan

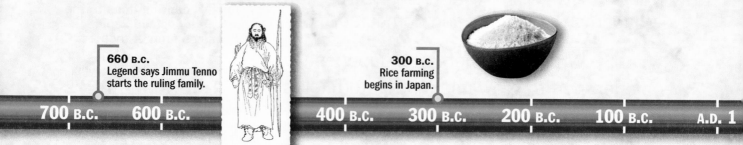

660 B.C.
Legend says Jimmu Tenno starts the ruling family.

300 B.C.
Rice farming begins in Japan.

700 B.C.   600 B.C.   400 B.C.   300 B.C.   200 B.C.   100 B.C.   A.D. 1

Why? Time lines can show events and eras of the near or the distant past. They help us understand when things happened. They also help us compare events.

How? Study the time line on these pages. The title tells what it is about. Notice which part of the time line shows B.C. and which part shows A.D. Find the place where B.C. ends and A.D. begins. Notice that the numbers get larger as you move to the left or right end of the time line. When you study the sections on the time line, you will notice that it is broken into centuries, or 100-year periods.

Think and Apply

1. Name one B.C. and one A.D. event on this time line.

2. When was rice farming introduced in Japan?

3. What is the most recent event on the time line?

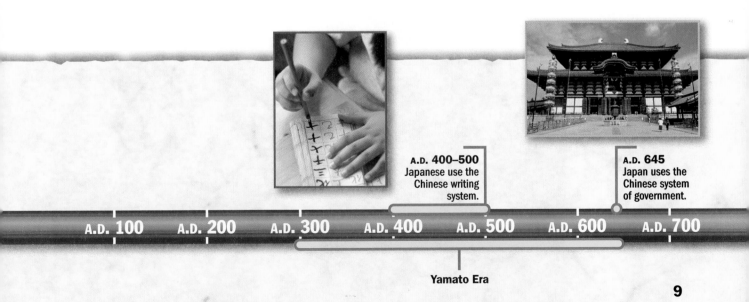

A.D. 400–500
Japanese use the Chinese writing system.

A.D. 645
Japan uses the Chinese system of government.

A.D. 100   A.D. 200   A.D. 300   A.D. 400   A.D. 500   A.D. 600   A.D. 700

Yamato Era

9

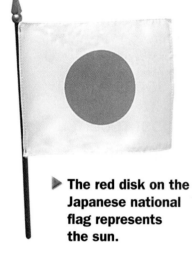

The Government of Japan

Today Japan still has an emperor. He is a symbol of the nation. Although the emperor is an important part of some ceremonies, he does not rule Japan.

Since World War II, Japan has had a democratic government. The prime minister is the leader of the national government. The people do not actually elect the prime minister. Instead, they vote for a political party. Then the winning party chooses a prime minister from among its members. Other advisors help the prime minister make decisions.

A group called the Diet (DY it) makes Japan's laws. It is made up of two houses like the United States Congress. The Diet has more than 700 elected members. Japan has a written set of rules, or constitution, by which the country is governed. This constitution was written after World War II. One part states that Japan cannot go to war with other countries unless it is attacked. This part of the constitution addresses the problems that war creates.

▶ The red disk on the Japanese national flag represents the sun.

▶ Emperor Akihito (shown with Empress Michiko) became emperor in 1989. The emperor is a living symbol of Japan.

The Supreme Court is Japan's highest court. The full Supreme Court is made up of fifteen judges. The Japanese court system does not have trials by jury as the United States does. Instead, a judge makes the decisions.

Just like our country is divided into areas of land called states, Japan is divided into areas of land called prefectures. Prefectures are ruled locally by a governor and representatives elected by the people. Smaller governments run cities, towns, or villages. They maintain parks, schools, and health services.

▶ **The Hiroshima Peace Memorial reminds the people of Japan of the problems that World War II caused. This strengthens their desire for peace.**

REVIEW Describe the roles of the emperor and the prime minister in Japan.

Main Ideas and Details

"And one morning I came in . . . , it was ten a.m. and General Whitney [head of the government section] called us into a meeting room. . . . [T]here were about 25 of us. And he said, 'You are now a constituent assembly [having the power to change a political constitution].' You can imagine how we felt. 'And you will write the Japanese constitution. You will write a draft and it will have to be done in a week.' Well, I mean, we were stunned of course. But . . . when you're in the army and you get an order, you just do it."

▶ A staff member for American General Douglas MacArthur remembers what it was like when she was given the order to help write Japan's new constitution.

DOCUMENT-BASED QUESTION *Describe how the staff member feels about writing Japan's constitution.*

The Economy of Japan

The economy of Japan suffered as a result of World War II. Many of Japan's cities, factories, and trading ships had been destroyed. Many people in Japan were out of work. Today Japan's economy has recovered and is very strong. Japan's economy is second only to that of the United States.

Most people in Japan have jobs. Factories keep many people working. Much of Japan's success is due to its exports, or what it sells to other countries.

Japan has few natural resources, so it must import natural resources from around the world. Japan imports, or buys, energy sources such as oil and coal and other raw materials. Then Japanese industries use the raw materials to make cars, radios, television sets, and computers. Japan exports motor vehicles and other manufactured goods, such as electronic equipment. Japan exports more goods than it imports.

DOCUMENT-BASED QUESTION

Look at the chart. What are some natural resources that Japan imports?

Imports	Exports
Oil	Autos
Textiles	Electronics
Liquid natural gas	Business machines
Audio-visual equipment	Optical instruments
Meat	Motor vehicle parts
Coal	Motors
Fish	Steel
	Chemicals
	Plastic materials

▶ **Thousands of tons of fish from countries all over the world are sold every day in the world's largest fish market, the Tsukiji Fish Market in Tokyo.**

Service industries are also important in Japan. Many people work for schools, banks, hospitals, and the government. Other people work in restaurants, research, and communications.

Few exports come from farming, forestry, fishing, or mining. The Japanese people are able to grow crops on only about one-seventh of Japan's land. Rice is an important crop. Japan is a leading fishing nation. Fish and shellfish are a large part of the Japanese diet.

▶ In a factory near Tokyo, a woman assembles a cell phone.

REVIEW Why does Japan import natural resources from around the world? **Main Idea and Details**

UNIT 1 ▶ **REVIEW AND ASSESS**

1. Copy the chart on a separate sheet of paper. Compare and contrast schools in Japan with schools in the United States.

Compare/Alike	Contrast/Different

2. Explain how the geography on each of Japan's four largest islands relates to the way people on those islands live.

3. How did contact with China and Korea change Japanese society?

4. How is Japan's system of government similar to and different from the United States' system of government?

5. Choose a product made in Japan, such as a car, TV, or computer. Create an advertisement to convince someone in the United States to buy the product.

Tying It All Together

How do the map on page 7, the quotation on page 11, and the chart on page 12 show that Japan has been influenced, or shaped, by contributions from other countries?

Touring Asia

The islands that form Japan are part of Asia. Asia has many countries. Here are some fun projects that can help you learn more about Asia.

TIGER

Asian Animal Cards

Make a card. Form a group to learn about the animals of Asia. Make a baseball-style card, illustrating your favorite Asian animal. Include facts about this animal. Swap animal cards with your friends.

The Stamps of Asia

Design a stamp. Suppose your job is to design postage stamps for an Asian country. Research the country you choose. Design a stamp that shows something special about the country you choose.

A Calendar of Asian Festivals

Make a calendar. Form a group to research some festivals celebrated in Asian countries. Make a calendar illustrating Asian festivals.

Asian Legends

Act out a legend. Many Asian countries have legends that tell made-up stories about past people. Legends are one way that people pass on values, ideas, beliefs, and traditions. Form a group. Research an Asian legend. Assign parts and make a mask for your character. Act out the legend for your class.

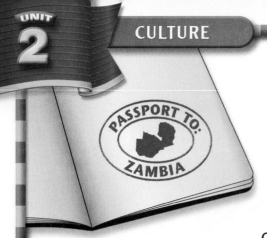

PASSPORT TO:
ZAMBIA

Welcome to Zambia!

My name is Teleza. I live in a rural area of eastern Zambia. Most people here are farmers. I go to the community school in the nearby city of Chipata. In the first years of school, I studied the language of my people. Now I learn English, which is the official language of my country. I also learn math, science, and social studies.

After school, I play soccer with my friends. I also help with chores at home. I have a big family, so I must help take care of my younger brothers and sisters.

Many people in Zambia follow traditional beliefs. Long ago my people were warriors. Some of our dances, songs, and celebrations honor the past. Each year in February we have a special ceremony called N'cwala. We give thanks for a good harvest. Dancers dress in animal skins and carry special wooden sticks. We honor our king by giving him the first fruits and vegetables of our harvest.

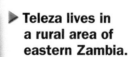

▶ **Teleza lives in a rural area of eastern Zambia.**

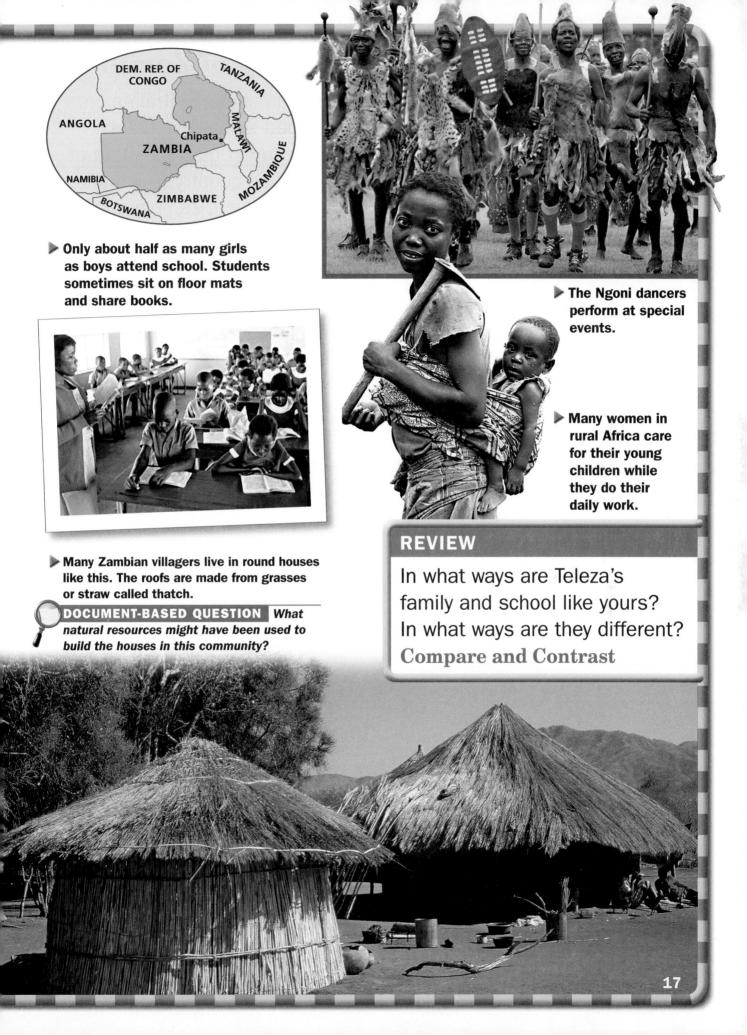

Only about half as many girls as boys attend school. Students sometimes sit on floor mats and share books.

Many Zambian villagers live in round houses like this. The roofs are made from grasses or straw called thatch.

DOCUMENT-BASED QUESTION *What natural resources might have been used to build the houses in this community?*

The Ngoni dancers perform at special events.

Many women in rural Africa care for their young children while they do their daily work.

REVIEW

In what ways are Teleza's family and school like yours? In what ways are they different?

Compare and Contrast

17

The Geography of Zambia

Zambia is located in south central Africa. The country is shaped somewhat like a butterfly. It is a little larger than the state of Texas. It is a landlocked country. This means it does not border an ocean. Zambia borders eight other countries.

Much of Zambia is a large plateau, or a high, flat land. The plateau is covered with forests. As rivers flow over the edges of the plateau, they form waterfalls. Mountains run across the plateau in the northeast. During the rainy season, a broad plain in the southwest floods.

▶ This satellite picture shows how some African lakes look from space. Find the part of this photo that matches the map below. The location of Mbala in the photo tells you that only northern Zambia is shown.

MAP SKILL

Zambia and Its Neighbors

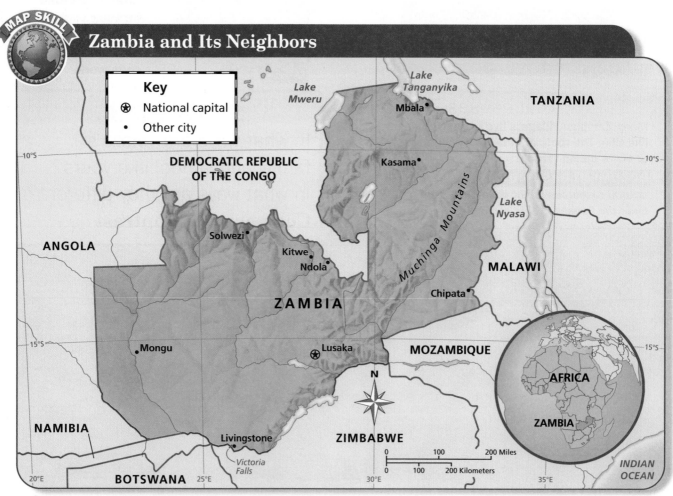

Key
⊛ National capital
• Other city

DEMOCRATIC REPUBLIC OF THE CONGO

Lake Mweru

Lake Tanganyika

TANZANIA

Mbala•

Kasama•

10°S

ANGOLA

Solwezi•

Kitwe•
Ndola•

Lake Nyasa

Muchinga Mountains

MALAWI

ZAMBIA

Chipata•

15°S

•Mongu

⊛ Lusaka

MOZAMBIQUE

N

AFRICA

ZAMBIA

NAMIBIA

Livingstone•

ZIMBABWE

0   100   200 Miles
0 100 200 Kilometers

INDIAN OCEAN

Victoria Falls

20°E   BOTSWANA   25°E

30°E

35°E

▶ Notice that eight countries border Zambia.

MAP SKILL Place *What two large lakes found on the map are shown in the photograph above?*

Zambia has a milder climate than some other places near the equator. This is because it is a plateau. Air temperature at high land is cooler than at low land. The rainy season lasts from November until April. The rest of the year can be very dry.

Zambia has many natural resources, such as copper, lead, and zinc. Natural features include forests and waterfalls. Elephants, lions, giraffes, and many other kinds of wildlife live there. Nineteen national parks have been set aside to protect the natural environment.

Over time, people in Zambia have changed the environment to meet their needs. They cleared forests so they could use the land for farming. They built dams and power stations on the rivers to produce electricity.

REVIEW What causes Zambia's climate to be milder than some other places located near the equator? **Cause and Effect**

▶ Visitors can walk through Luangwa National Park. It is home to 60 different kinds of animals and 400 different kinds of birds.

▶ Baobab (BAY oh bab) trees are found on Zambia's grasslands. People can eat the fruit and make rope from the bark.

▶ Mists from the 300-foot high Victoria Falls can be seen for miles. Zambians call it "the smoke that thunders."

19

Use Latitude and Longitude

What? **Latitude lines,** also called parallels, are imaginary lines that circle the Earth. They measure distances in degrees (°) north (N) and south (S) of the equator. The equator (0°) is the largest latitude line. Latitude lines are numbered from 0° to 90°. On the left globe below, the lines are at 20° intervals.

Longitude lines, also called meridians, are similar to latitude lines. However, they measure distances in degrees east (E) and west (W) of the prime meridian.

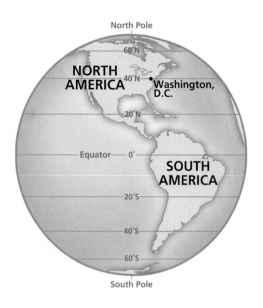

Latitude

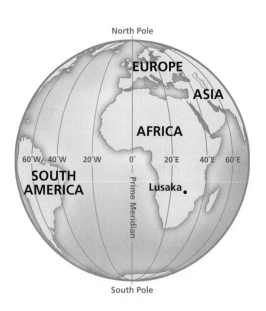

Longitude

Longitude lines go from the North Pole to the South Pole. The **prime meridian** is the starting point for measuring these degrees from 0° to 180°. The globe at the bottom right of page 20 is marked at 20° intervals.

Why? The lines of latitude and longitude on the same map or globe will cross each other to form a grid. You can use the grid to find the location of places on maps and globes. You can locate cities, countries, continents, and oceans.

How? Lusaka is the capital of Zambia. Imagine that the latitude lines of the left globe were placed on the longitude globe. Lusaka would be just above the 20°S latitude line, or at about 15°S.

Lusaka is also about halfway between the 20°E and 40°E longitude lines, or at about 30°E. So the city of Lusaka is located about 15°S, 30°E. When giving a location, always give latitude degrees first.

Think and Apply

1 Look at the globes on page 20. What is the name of the line of latitude that is labeled 0°? What is the name of the line of longitude that is labeled 0°?

2 Which location is closer to the equator—a place located at 20°S or a place located at 40°S?

3 Look at the globes on page 20. Washington, D.C., is located almost exactly on which line of latitude? Between which two lines of longitude is the city of Lusaka located?

The History of Zambia

People have lived in what is now Zambia for many thousands of years. Some scientists believe that about 15,000 years ago, people lived in caves in the region. They gathered fruits and honey for food. They made and used weapons to hunt for animals.

About 1,500 years ago, Bantu (BAHN too), or black African people, migrated to what is now Zambia. The Bantu developed civilizations. A civilization is an advanced way of life with organized systems of government, religion, and learning. The Bantu mined iron and copper. They made tools and weapons. The Bantu also farmed the land.

Between A.D. 1500 and 1800, the region of what is now Zambia divided into kingdoms. These kingdoms traded copper and ivory with other peoples in Africa. In the mid-1700s, traders from Portugal came to Zambia. They shipped enslaved Africans to faraway places.

Iron	Copper
Hunting	Jewelry
Farming	Money

▶ These artifacts give us clues about how people in Africa lived long ago.

DOCUMENT-BASED QUESTION

State two ways ancient people in Africa used materials from their environment.

History of Zambia

Ancient Zambia

About 13,000 B.C.
People gather food and hunt.

Later History of Zambia

About A.D. 500
Bantu migrate to what is now Zambia.

13,000 B.C.   A.D. 1   A.D. 500

One person who wanted to end the African slave trade was David Livingstone. He was a missionary, or a person sent into an area to do certain kinds of work. Livingstone came from Britain to explore southern Africa in the mid-1800s. He wanted Africans to grow cotton for trade with Britain. He believed this would help end the practice of selling enslaved people to work in cotton fields in the Americas. Livingstone died before he could carry out his plan, but others continued his work.

In the late 1800s, what is now Zambia became a British colony. The slave trade ended, but life did not improve for black Africans who worked in the mines.

Africans began to work for freedom from British rule. In the late 1950s, Africans formed a group that worked to win more rights for blacks. In 1964 Zambia became an independent country. Kenneth Kaunda (kah OON dah) became its first president.

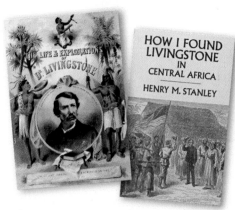

▶ **David Livingstone wrote about his own life (autobiography) and others wrote about him (biography). These books have helped people understand what Africa was like in the mid-1800s.**

▶ **On the Zambian flag, the green background stands for the land. The red stripe stands for freedom. The black stripe stands for the people. The orange stripe stands for mineral wealth, especially copper. The eagle stands for freedom.**

REVIEW Discuss several ways that David Livingstone was important to Africa.
Draw Conclusions

A.D. 1500–1800
Region is divided into kingdoms.

About A.D. 1750
Portuguese traders arrive.

About A.D. 1850
Livingstone works to end slave trade.

About A.D. 1880
European nations divide Africa among themselves.

About A.D. 1950
Groups form to fight for rights for blacks.

A.D. 1964
Zambia gains independence.

A.D. **1000**   A.D. **1500**   A.D. **2000**

Facts about Zambia

Official Name:	Republic of Zambia
Population:	9,959,037 (2002 est.)
Largest Cities:	Lusaka, Kitwe, Ndola
Monetary Unit:	Kwacha
Languages:	English and about 70 native languages

The Government of Zambia

President Kaunda remained in office for 27 years. He supported education and worked to improve the economy. He took control of Zambia's mining industry. Life for most people did not improve. Many believed Kaunda limited people's rights. As a result, Kaunda was voted out of office when free elections were held in 1991.

Today Zambia is a republic. In a republic, citizens have the right to choose their leaders. As in the United States, voters in Zambia elect the president and the lawmakers. All citizens 18 years of age and older can vote. The constitution gives all citizens equal rights under the law.

Ethnic groups in Zambia also still honor their traditional leaders. Zambian chiefs and kings make day-to-day decisions that affect their people. These leaders, however, are not part of Zambia's government.

REVIEW What kind of government does Zambia now have? **Main Idea and Details**

▶ **Zambian citizens vote to elect their leaders.**

Reshaping a Nation

The country of South Africa has a long history of conflicts between white people and black people. In 1948 the government of South Africa passed laws to separate white people from all other ethnic groups. This system of laws was called apartheid (uh PART hayt).

White leaders in South Africa believed that white people should control the country. Black people were forced to live apart from white people. Blacks could not vote or take part in government. People who fought against apartheid were harshly punished.

Many people disagreed with the government of South Africa. Students, religious groups, and others organized protests against apartheid. Countries joined together and agreed not to trade with South Africa.

Zambia became a leader in the fight against apartheid. Zambians believed that all people should be treated fairly. Africans from other countries fled to Zambia to escape the harsh conditions in their own countries.

Apartheid ended in 1990. South Africa held its first free election in 1994. Nelson Mandela became the country's first black president.

"America's view of apartheid is simple. . . . We believe it is wrong. . . . And we are united in hoping for the day when apartheid will be no more."

Ronald Reagan, President of the United States 1981–1989

"Today we have closed the book on apartheid."

F. W. de Klerk, president of South Africa 1989–1994

"Education is the most powerful weapon which you can use to change the world."

Nelson Mandela, president of South Africa 1994–1999

Issues and You

How do you think the long struggle to end apartheid affected the lives of people in South Africa?

The Economy of Zambia

Many people in Zambia struggle to make a living. The government used to control Zambia's economy. Other countries did not invest in Zambia's industries because they could not make a profit.

Demands in world markets also affected Zambia's economy. Copper has always been Zambia's most important export. Changing technology decreased the demand for copper. When the demand for a product decreases, the price of the product often decreases. The price of copper fell, and Zambia's economy suffered.

How Zambia uses its resources is important to its economic growth. Only a small amount of Zambia's land is used for farming. Corn, cotton, sugarcane, tobacco, wheat, coffee, and tea all grow well in Zambia. One goal of Zambia's government is to increase the amount of land used for farming. Large farms could produce crops for export.

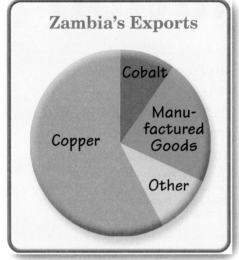

Zambia's Exports

▶ Copper and cobalt are mined from the earth. Manufactured goods are made in factories.

DOCUMENT-BASED QUESTION

How does this chart show the importance of natural resources to Zambia's economy?

▶ A large electric shovel loads trucks at a copper mine in Zambia.

Today Zambia's government does not control its industries. It is easier for companies to make profits. Manufacturing is becoming more important to Zambia's economy. Copper wire and cable are some products made in Zambia.

Tourism is also important to Zambia's economy. Visitors from all over the world come to see Victoria Falls. Many people visit Zambia's national parks. Tourists enjoy the festivals of different cultures in Zambia.

▶ **Tourism is a growing business in Zambia.**

REVIEW What are several reasons why many people in Zambia struggle to make a living? **Summarize**

UNIT 2 ◀ REVIEW AND ASSESS

1. Draw a diagram like the one shown. Fill in the details that support the main idea.

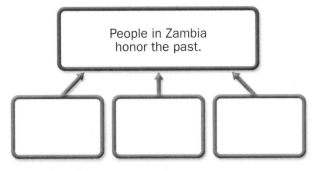

People in Zambia honor the past.

2. How do people in Zambia modify the environment to meet their needs?

3. Sequence five important events in the history of Zambia.

4. Why did apartheid cause conflicts in South Africa?

5. Suppose you are on a photography safari in Zambia. Write a postcard telling friends about the land and animals you have seen.

Tying It All Together

Based on the picture of the houses on page 17, the artifacts on page 22, and the graph on page 26, explain how people in Zambia have used the country's natural resources.

Touring Africa

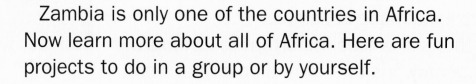

Zambia is only one of the countries in Africa. Now learn more about all of Africa. Here are fun projects to do in a group or by yourself.

Who's Who in Africa?

Learn from biographies and autobiographies. Find out more about David Livingstone. What parts of Africa did he explore? Why did Henry Stanley go to Africa to look for Livingstone? What did Stanley say when he found him? Tell how reading about Livingstone's life helps you understand the time and place in which he lived.

Civilization in the Desert

Find out about Egypt. Form a group. Locate Egypt on a map. Find out about the great civilization that developed there thousands of years ago. Why did the people build pyramids? Make models or sculptures to show what Egypt's ancient culture was like. Make a display for your class.

Tell a Story

Read African folktales. Many African folktales tell about animals. Many are meant to teach a value or tradition. Choose one of these stories from your school or local library. Practice it until you know it well. Then tell it to the class. Explain what lesson you think the folktale was meant to teach.

Traveling the World

Locate continents and oceans. Work with a group. Find a map or globe that shows lines of latitude and longitude. Which continents are closest to Africa? Name the continents the equator or prime meridian passes through. Next find the oceans closest to Africa. Name the oceans that the equator or prime meridian passes over. Make a papier-mâché model of the globe and label the continents and oceans.

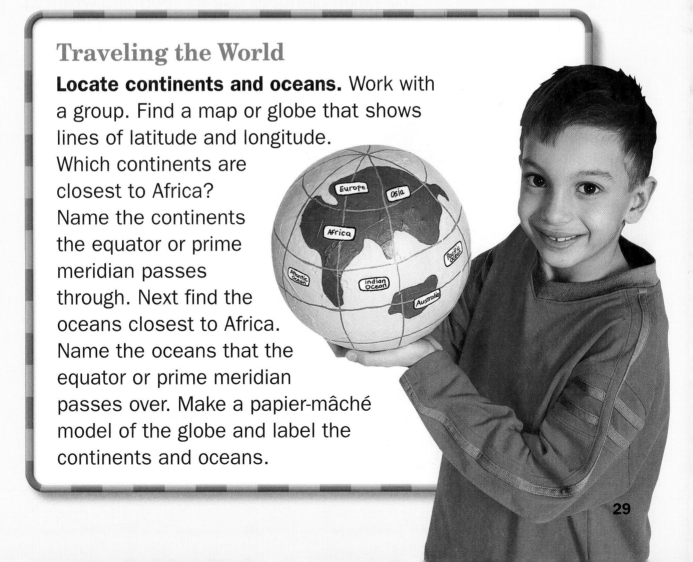

Welcome to Brazil!

Hello! My name is Paulinho. I live in the rain forest along the Amazon River in Brazil. The rain forest provides most of the things we need to live. I am a member of the Kayapo Indian group. Let me tell you about my culture.

I do not go to a school as you do. The older Kayapo people teach me the things I need to know to live in the rain forest. They teach me skills such as fishing and hunting. They teach me how to take care of myself. They even teach me which plants to use for food and which to use for medicine. My people need to know these skills in order to survive.

The men and boys in the group hunt and fish. The men also maintain peace in the village and plan ceremonies. The women cook and tend the gardens.

Body painting is a tradition in Kayapo culture. The painting tells a story about the person wearing it. What do you think the paint on my face tells about me?

▶ Paulinho is nine years old. His Kayapo ancestors have lived in the rain forest for thousands of years.

Amazon rain forest

PERU
PACIFIC OCEAN
BOLIVIA
BRAZIL
PARAGUAY
ATLANTIC OCEAN
ARGENTINA
URUGUAY

▶ Rain forest birds called toucans have very large bills.

▶ The Amazon River is the second longest river in the world.

▶ Kayapo men use palm branches in building their houses.

▶ In most Kayapo villages, the houses form a circle. The men meet in a house in the center of the circle.

REVIEW

How do the Kayapo learn about the beliefs, customs, and traditions of their people?
Main Idea and Details

The Geography of Brazil

Brazil is the largest country in South America, covering almost half the continent. It is divided into five geographic regions: the Northeast, North, Central-West, Southeast, and South.

The Northeast region has some of Brazil's most beautiful beaches. Although there is an area of rich farmland along the coast, most of this region is rocky and gets very little rainfall. When it does rain, the region often floods. The dry spells and flooding cause people to migrate to other parts of Brazil.

▶ **Brightly colored tropical plants are found in Brazil.**

The Regions of Brazil

Key
- ✪ National capital
- • Other cities

Vegetation Key
- Dense forest
- Mixed forest
- Grassland

▶ The physical characteristics of each region in Brazil are very different.

MAP SKILL Use Map Scale *About how many miles is it from the capital city, Brasília, to Rio de Janeiro?*

The North region is home to the world's largest tropical rain forest and the mighty Amazon River. This region, the country's largest, covers almost half of Brazil, but it has a small population.

The Central-West region is known for its huge cattle ranches. A swampy area called the Pantanal (PAHN tuh NAHL) is in this region. So is the nation's capital city, Brasilia.

There are mountains and farmland in the most developed region, the Southeast. The cities of São Paulo and Rio de Janeiro, where most of the people of Brazil live, are also located here.

The South is the smallest region. Cattle roam on pastures called *pampas* that dot the landscape. Rocky coasts, forests, and waterfalls are also found here.

REVIEW   Name and describe the five regions of Brazil.
Main Idea and Details

▶ Iguaçu Falls is on the border of Brazil and Argentina.

Literature and Social Studies

Nature's Green Umbrella

Natural resources are limited, but people's needs and wants are not. Author Gail Gibbons traveled to several rain forests to research her book *Nature's Green Umbrella: Tropical Rain Forests*. In the book, she explores the importance of tropical rain forests, as well as threats to their existence. She writes about these historic changes.

For most of their existence, the tropical rain forests were left undisturbed. Rain forest plants and animals flourished. Today many rain forests are quickly disappearing. . . . Trees are being harvested for their valuable wood. Even more are being cut down and burned to clear the land for roads, farming, and grazing. This practice is called "slash and burn."

– Gail Gibbons, *Nature's Green Umbrella: Tropical Rain Forests*, New York: Morrow, William & Co., 1994.

DOCUMENT-BASED QUESTION
Why are the tropical rain forests disappearing?

Use a Pie Chart

What? You have learned that Brazil has different kinds of land. Some land is good for farming. Some land is covered by forests. Look at the pie chart below. It shows the different ways Brazil uses its land. A **pie chart**, or circle graph, looks like a pie that is cut into pieces. A pie chart is used to compare parts of a whole.

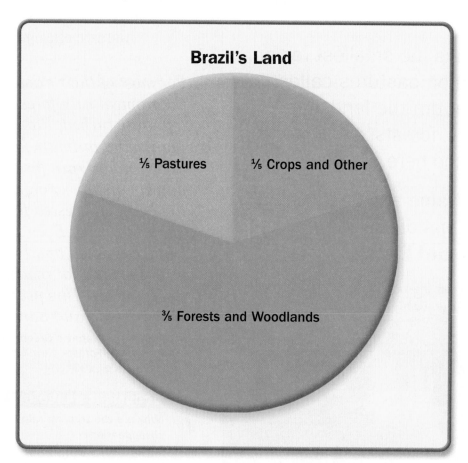

Brazil's Land

⅕ Pastures

⅕ Crops and Other

⅗ Forests and Woodlands

Why? A pie chart can help you see how parts relate to one another. It shows you which part is the biggest and which part is the smallest.

How? When you read a pie chart, look at the title. The title tells you what the "whole" pie chart stands for. Then look at the name and fraction shown for each "piece" of the pie. You will be able to see how the pieces relate to each other. The fractions will add up to the number one. Check them to make sure they do.

Think and Apply

1. How much of Brazil's land is used for crops or other things?

2. What valuable resource covers about ⅗ of the country?

3. How much more land is covered with forests than is used for pastures?

The History of Brazil

Indians were the first inhabitants of the land we now call Brazil. Then, in 1500, an explorer named Pedro Álvares Cabral (PAY droh AHL vahr ehs cah BRAHL) arrived on Brazil's shores. He claimed the land for Portugal.

The Portuguese soon began immigrating to Brazil. At first the new settlers cut down trees and exported the brazilwood back to Portugal. Then they began raising sugarcane. The settlers needed people to work in the sugar fields, so they enslaved Indians. Then Portugal began to bring people from Africa to do more of the work.

▶ **In the early 1800s an artist created this illustration of workers in a small sugar mill.**

🔍 DOCUMENT-BASED QUESTION

What are two ways sugarcane plants could be transported to this sugar mill for processing?

Many modern sugar mills use water to produce the electricity they need.

The discovery of gold and diamonds attracted thousands more Portuguese to Brazil. People also immigrated to grow coffee or cotton. Many became cattle ranchers.

Portugal ruled Brazil until 1822, when Brazil became an independent nation. In 1888, a law ended slavery. Brazil became a republic in 1889. Immigrants from other parts of Europe poured into Brazil. They came to work on farms and in mines in place of the enslaved people.

REVIEW Why were there more jobs in Brazil for European immigrants after 1888?
Cause and Effect

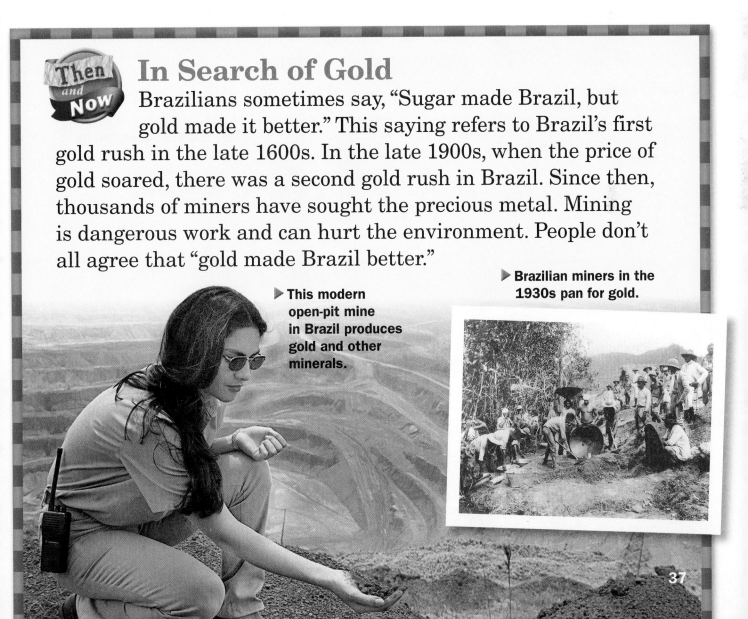

Then and Now

In Search of Gold

Brazilians sometimes say, "Sugar made Brazil, but gold made it better." This saying refers to Brazil's first gold rush in the late 1600s. In the late 1900s, when the price of gold soared, there was a second gold rush in Brazil. Since then, thousands of miners have sought the precious metal. Mining is dangerous work and can hurt the environment. People don't all agree that "gold made Brazil better."

▶ This modern open-pit mine in Brazil produces gold and other minerals.

▶ Brazilian miners in the 1930s pan for gold.

37

The Government of Brazil

The first constitution of Brazil was created in 1891. Like the United States Constitution, it calls for three branches of government—the executive, the legislative, and the judicial. The president is head of the executive branch and has many powers. The president chooses cabinet members to help in making decisions. Other groups give the president advice too.

The legislative branch, or the Congress, makes the laws. Similar to those of Canada and the United States, Brazil's Congress has two houses. Both the Federal Senate and the Chamber of Deputies are made up of people elected from the twenty-six states and the federal district of Brazil.

▶ Just as United States citizens do, Brazilians vote for a president every four years. They also elect members of Congress.

▶ This building, designed by Brazilian architect Oscar Niemeyer, is where Congress meets.

The courts make up the judicial branch. The Supreme Federal Tribunal is the highest court in Brazil. The president appoints judges to this court, but each judge must be approved by the Senate. The court decides whether laws are fair and settles disagreements over rules, rights, and responsibilities.

In Brazil, a law requires that all people between the ages of eighteen and seventy who can read and write must vote. Are citizens of our country required to vote?

▶ **The flag of Brazil**

REVIEW Which branch of government settles conflicts? **Main Idea and Details**

FACT FILE

Brasilia

Brazil has had three capital cities: Salvador, Rio de Janeiro, and Brasilia. Two famous Brazilian designers planned Brasilia, the current capital. If you looked down on the city from above, you would see it is shaped like an airplane. You would see that government offices make up the center cabin of the plane. The executive, legislative, and judicial buildings form the nose of the plane, and the parts of the city where most of the people live form the wings. Brasilia was created to encourage people to move inland, and that is just what they did.

▶ **You can see the shape of Brasilia in this satellite image.**

PASSPORT TO: BRAZIL

The Economy of Brazil

You know that Brazil has and develops many natural resources. It mines metals and gems and harvests trees. It also grows sugarcane, coffee, and cotton, as well as rice, nuts, wheat, and corn. Other agricultural products that contribute to Brazil's economic growth include rubber, citrus fruit, and avocados.

People in other parts of the world need these products. Brazil sells, or exports, these products to other countries. Brazil buys, or imports, products that it does not have, such as oil, coal, and chemicals. Like all societies, Brazil must make economic decisions about which goods and services to produce and which to import.

Brazil also manufactures products. It makes airplanes, trucks, and tractors. It makes clothing, shoes, tires, electric appliances, and machinery. More than half of Brazil's exports come from goods people make in factories.

► Wood products help Brazil's economy. This logging camp is located along the Amazon River.

DOCUMENT-BASED QUESTION

When did coffee become a major export in Brazil?

Brazil's Major Exports

1500	1600	1700
1500s Sugarcane	**1600s** Sugarcane	**1700s** Gold, Diamonds

Although Brazil is a wealthy country, not everyone in Brazil is rich. In fact, many Brazilians make very little money. However, the middle class is growing. People in service industries, such as teachers and health-care workers, now make up a large part of Brazil's work force.

▶ The *real* is Brazil's basic unit of money. It has been in use since 1994.

REVIEW What does Brazil export and import? **Main Idea and Details**

UNIT 3 ◀ REVIEW AND ASSESS

1. Why do members of the Kayapo Indian group learn skills such as which plants to use for food and medicine?

2. Why do you think that the North region has a small population even though it covers a large area?

3. Why did Portugese and other European immigrants come to Brazil? What effect did they have?

4. Name the three branches of the Brazilian government and explain their functions.

5. Create an advertisement to attract people to Brazil. Describe its resources and how the country uses them for economic growth.

Tying It All Together

Based on the literature selection on page 33, the photograph on page 36, and the time line on pages 40–41, explain how Brazil uses its natural resources.

1800

1900

2000

1800s
Coffee

1900s
Coffee and Rubber

2000s
Iron Ore

Touring South America

Brazil is only one of the countries in South America. Now learn more about all of South America. Here are fun projects to do alone or in a group.

Chart It

Make a chart.
Form a group. Read an informational book about a country in South America. Create a chart that shows what you learned about landforms, animals, and holidays in that country. Display your chart in the classroom.

	Chile	Argentina	Uruguay
Landforms	Andes Mts.	The Pampa	
Animals	Llama	Armadillo	
Holidays			Carnival Week

Wave the Flag

Design a flag. Research flags of South American countries. Use art supplies to create one of the flags. Describe your flag to the class.

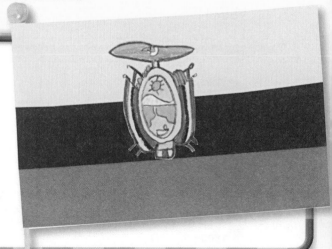

Dear Journal

Write experiences. Pretend you are traveling through a country in South America. Research the country you chose. Write a journal entry about what happens during one day of your trip.

Celebrate!

Create a diorama. Form a group. Research South American festivals. Make a scene showing a festival. Share your diorama with the class.

Welcome to Spain!

Hello! My name is Marita. I live in Cádiz, on the southwest coast of Spain. I live with my parents and brother Luis in an apartment.

On school days, I get up at 6:30 A.M. After I get dressed, I have cereal and milk for breakfast. Then I walk to school. I attend a public state school. When my school day ends at 1:30 P.M., I gather my books and walk home.

During my father's work break at 2:30 P.M., he comes home for lunch. In Spain, lunch is the main meal of the day. After lunch I study. Then we have a small dinner around 9:00 P.M. My favorite dinner is pizza!

In February we enjoy two days of vacation from school for Carnival. Carnival is a week-long festival near the end of winter. Cádiz has one of the most colorful Carnivals in Spain.

▶ Marita is nine years old. She lives in Cádiz, one of the oldest cities in Spain.

The peninsula that Spain shares with Portugal is called the Iberian Peninsula.

Paella is a Spanish dish made with rice, chicken, seafood, and vegetables.

The Carnival in Cádiz is like Mardi Gras in New Orleans, Louisiana.

Students in Spain have many things in common with students in the United States.

Cádiz is on the Atlantic Ocean. Marita's family likes to go to the beach.

REVIEW

How is Marita's day like yours? How is it different?

Compare and Contrast

The Geography of Spain

If you visit Spain, you will notice that it has several regions. The largest region is in the middle of the country. It is a dry plateau, or high, flat area, called the Meseta. You might see sheep and cattle there, but few people. Most of the people in the Meseta region live in or near Madrid, Spain's capital city.

Several mountain ranges surround the Meseta. In the northern mountain region, you will find the rugged Pyrenees. They separate Spain from the part of Europe to its north.

▶ **Sheep can be seen on the Meseta.**

MAP SKILL

Spain

44°N — Bay of Biscay
FRANCE
ANDORRA
•Bilbao
Cantabrian Mountains
42°N
Ebro River
P y r e n e e s

Key
⊛ National capital
• Other cities

ATLANTIC OCEAN
Duero River
Barcelona•
Mediterranean Sea
PORTUGAL
SPAIN
Madrid ⊛
M E S E T A
Balearic Islands (SPAIN)
40°N
Tagus River
•Toledo
Valencia•
Guadiana River

38°N
Guadalquivur River
•Córdoba
Seville•
Granada•
Sierra Nevada
N
SPAIN EUROPE
•Cádiz
36°N
To the Canary Islands (SPAIN)
Strait of Gibraltar
10°W   8°W   6°W   4°W   2°W   0°   2°E   4°E   6°E

0   50   100 Miles
0   50   100 Kilometers

▶ **Madrid, Spain's largest city, is located in the mostly flat Meseta region.**

DOCUMENT-BASED QUESTION | *What large country is separated from Spain by the Pyrenees?*

Spain's coasts are narrow lowlands squeezed between mountain ranges and the water. Farmers in this region grow fruits, vegetables, and grains. Dry, sunny summers bring tourists to the beaches and resorts. As a tourist you would see cities and many people in the coastal areas.

REVIEW Name three of Spain's geographical regions. Tell one feature of each region. **Main Idea and Details**

▶ Olive trees can be found growing on the Meseta.

▶ **Cattle graze on the Meseta.**

Literature and Social Studies

The Meseta

American writer Washington Irving wrote his book *The Alhambra* after a visit to Spain in 1829. Here he writes about the Meseta.

In ranging over these boundless wastes, the eye catches sight here and there of cattle attended by a lonely herdsman, motionless as a statue . . . or beholds a long train of mules slowly moving along the waste like a train of camels in the desert . . . .

🔍 **DOCUMENT-BASED QUESTION**
How does Washington Irving describe the people who work on the Meseta?

47

Use a Population Density Map

What? You have been reading about regions of Spain. You have learned that some regions have many people, and other regions have few people. A **population density map** shows how population is spread out over an area. An area where a lot of people live is densely populated. If an area has few people living in it, it is lightly populated.

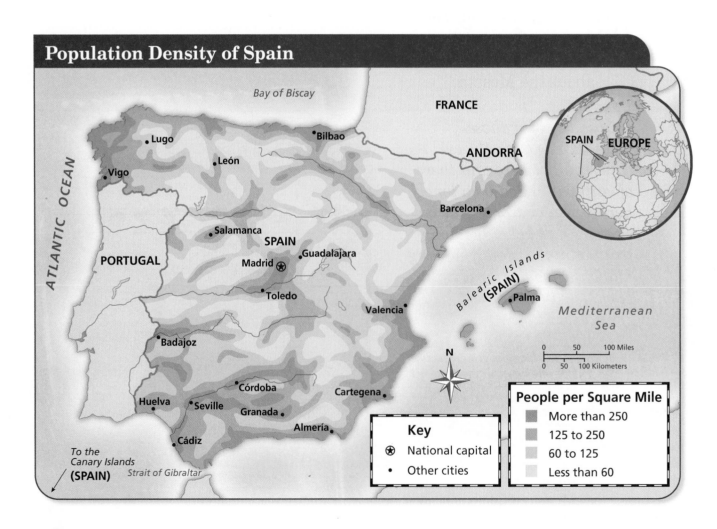

Population Density of Spain

Key

⊛ National capital

• Other cities

People per Square Mile

More than 250

125 to 250

60 to 125

Less than 60

Why? A population density map shows how geography affects where people live. You have read that most people from the Meseta live in Madrid. You have also learned that many people live in cities along Spain's coasts. This information is shown on the map.

How? Each color on the map represents the number of people living in one square mile. To understand a square mile, picture a large square drawn on land in which each side measures one mile. Places with the most people per square mile are the most densely populated. Which parts of Spain are the most densely populated?

Look at the map key on page 48. Yellow stands for places with fewer than 60 people per square mile. Find the places that are yellow on the map. These places are lightly populated.

Think and Apply

❶ What is a population density map?

❷ Which place has about the same population density as Cádiz—Barcelona or Lugo? How can you tell?

❸ Compare the map on page 48 with the map on page 46. Why do you think few people live in the area of Spain that borders France and Andorra?

▶ This satellite image shows lights from cities in Spain. How does it show where most people live?

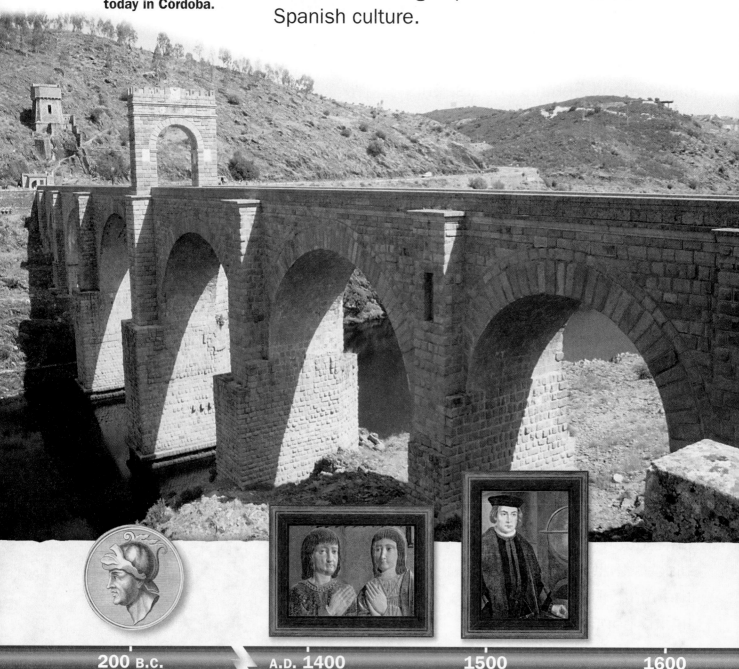

PASSPORT TO: SPAIN

The History of Spain

In the past, several groups ruled the land that became Spain. The Romans ruled for about 600 years. After the Romans, tribes from northern Europe invaded. Then the Moors, a group of Muslims from Africa, ruled. All these groups had an effect on Spanish culture.

▶ **This bridge first built by the ancient Romans is still in use today in Córdoba.**

200 B.C. A.D. 1400 1500 1600

about 200 B.C. Romans begin to rule the land that became Spain.

1469 King Ferdinand and Queen Isabella get married.

1492 Queen Isabella sponsors the first voyage of Christopher Columbus.

By 1492 King Ferdinand and Queen Isabella had united Spain and conquered the Moors. Spain became a Christian country. The Spanish Empire grew and became very powerful. Spanish explorers claimed huge areas of the Americas.

Slowly, Spain's powerful empire fell apart. It began to lose control of its colonies. Then in 1898 Spain fought the Spanish-American War with the United States. When the war was over, Spain gave the last of its colonies in the Americas to the United States.

In the 1930s Spain had a bloody civil war. After the war, General Franco became dictator. When Franco died in 1975, Juan Carlos was made king. He is still head of Spain's elected government.

▶ In 1656 Diego Velázquez painted this picture of little Princess Margarita of Spain and her ladies in waiting.

REVIEW What effect did King Ferdinand and Queen Isabella have on Spain?
Cause and Effect

1700	1800	1900	2000
1779 Spanish troops invade Florida.	**1833** Isabella II becomes queen of Spain.	**1898** Spanish-American War is fought.	**1975** Juan Carlos becomes king of Spain.

The Government of Spain

Today Spain is a democratic country. It has a constitution that went into effect in 1978. Like the citizens of the United States, the citizens of Spain have rights. They choose their leaders by voting in elections.

An elected president directs the national government of Spain. The president has duties similar to those of the President of the United States. The king is head of state in Spain. These leaders work together to govern Spain.

▶ **The Royal Palace is located in Spain's capital, Madrid. King Juan Carlos and his family do not live in the palace, but use it for special events.**

52

Spain has a parliament and a Supreme Court. The parliament is like the United States Congress. Members of parliament are elected by the people. Spain's national government is located in Madrid.

Spain also has 17 large areas, each with its own government. Each area elects leaders to solve local problems.

Spain is a member of the European Union, an organization of 15 European countries. These countries work together in many areas, such as economics, law enforcement, and foreign policy.

▶ **King Juan Carlos and Queen Sophia represent Spain at important events around the world.**

REVIEW How are the governments of Spain and the United States alike? How are they different? **Compare and Contrast**

FACT FILE

Flag of Spain

There are many stories about the symbols on the Spanish flag. Some say the lion symbol is the same one the Roman armies used. The white pillars are said to represent the Pillars of Hercules, the land on either side of the Strait of Gibraltar. The motto *Plus ultra* means "More beyond." It probably refers to the discoveries by Spanish explorers. Today a crown tops the shield. The crown honors the role of the king or queen in modern Spain.

▶ **Detail of the crest from the flag of Spain.**

▶ **Flag of Spain**

The Economy of Spain

From the 1950s until the early 1970s, Spain had a troubled economy. Many people were very poor. Farmers had a hard time making a living. Many people moved to the cities looking for work. Thousands left Spain and got jobs in other European countries.

When Juan Carlos became king, the government made many changes. Spain's economy began to improve. Workers returned to Spain. They bought houses and started businesses. Some people went back to their villages. They started modern farms. They began to grow food to sell in the supermarkets of Europe.

▶ Grapes are harvested in Spain's vineyards.

Products of Spain	Where They Are Produced
Iron, coal, minerals	Northern mountain regions
Fruits, vegetables, grains	Coastal regions
Automobiles	Cities of Madrid, Barcelona, Valencia
Fish	Atlantic Ocean, Mediterranean Sea
Grapes	Northern part of the Meseta, coastal regions
Electronics and technology	Barcelona, Madrid, and surrounding areas

DOCUMENT-BASED QUESTION Where does most of Spain's mining take place?

▶ Olive groves are important to Spain's economy.

Other parts of Spain's economy also improved. For example, Spain has become a large producer of automobiles. It sells most of its cars to other countries in Europe. Spain is a leading producer of iron ore and coal. It is also one of the largest producers of olives, citrus fruits, and cork.

Tourism is very important to Spain's economy. Many people from other countries escape cold winters by going to the beaches in Spain.

▶ **Spanish factories produce many automobiles.**

REVIEW Compare the economy of Spain before and after Juan Carlos became king. **Compare and Contrast**

UNIT 4 ◀ REVIEW AND ASSESS

1. What are two ways in which daily life in Cádiz, Spain, is different from daily life in your community?

2. What body of water borders the east coast of Spain?

3. Make a time line that shows the important dates and events in Spain's history.

4. Why is it important that citizens of a country have rights, such as the right to choose their leaders?

5. Suppose you are Juan Carlos, and you have just been made king of Spain. Write a journal entry that describes the problems in the country's economy and what you will do to bring change.

Tying It All Together

Based on the map on page 46, Washington Irving's description on page 47, and the chart on page 54, how has geography affected the lives of the Spanish people?

Touring Europe

Spain is only one of the countries in Europe. Now learn more about all of Europe. Here are fun projects to do in a group or by yourself.

How High Is It?

Draw a map. Form a group. Find a physical map of Europe. Make sure that the map key shows a mountain peak. Working with your group, draw a map that shows where three of the highest mountains in Europe are located.

Let's Play!

Demonstrate a sport. Form a group. Research sports that people play in Spain and in the rest of Europe. Choose a sport to study. Show the class how to play the sport. Use real equipment if you can.

Belgium

Switzerland

Scotland

Made in Europe

Research goods. Form a group. Find pictures of products from Europe that are sold in the United States. Make a display of the pictures. Label each product to tell where it is made. Present your display to the class.

Greetings!

Write a postcard. Suppose you are a tourist in Spain or in another country in Europe. Using technology and library resources, research the country you chose. Make a postcard you might send. Draw a picture showing something about the country you chose. Write a note on the back.

Welcome to Australia!

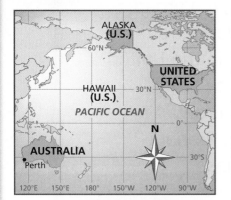

G'Day, mate! That is how we say "Hello, friend!" in Australia. My name is Dan. I live in Perth, on the southwest coast of Australia. The weather here is warm and sunny, so we enjoy being outdoors. My parents take me swimming in the Indian Ocean with my sister, Tasha. We moved to this community because my father works for the Department of Mineral Resources. Once he drove us to visit a gold-mining site east of Perth. We passed wheat, sheep, and dairy farms.

I attend school from 9:00 A.M. to 3:15 P.M. every weekday. My school has four terms during the year. We have two-week breaks between terms. In December we begin a six-week summer vacation.

We celebrate our national day, Australia Day, on January 26 by having parades, barbecues, and fireworks. We remember when the British first settled in Australia. In February we have the Chinese New Year's parade and festival.

▶ **Dan lives in Perth, a city located at the far western edge of Australia.**

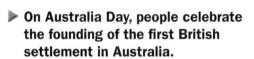

▶ Perth is in Western Australia. It is far from any other major Australian city.

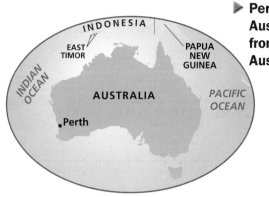

▶ On Australia Day, people celebrate the founding of the first British settlement in Australia.

▶ The mild climate near Perth is good for sheep, dairy, and grain farms. The area also has mines and forests.

▶ Children enjoy playing the game *cricket*. A cricket bat is flat, not round like a baseball bat.

▶ Perth is a good place to enjoy the outdoors. Many families sail boats or swim at Perth's beaches.

REVIEW

How is Dan's school like yours? How is it different?
Compare and Contrast

The Geography of Australia

Australia, which is called "The Land Down Under," is the only country that is also a continent. It is located "down under" the equator, in the Southern Hemisphere. Southern Hemisphere seasons are the opposite of seasons in the Northern Hemisphere. When it is winter in Australia, it is summer in the United States.

Most Australians live in cities along the north, east, and southwest coasts. These coastal plains have good rivers and plentiful rainfall. The Great Dividing Range is a long mountain region.

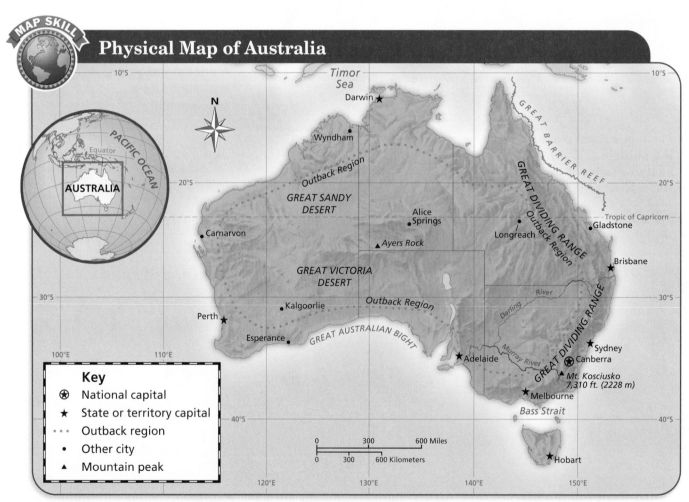

Physical Map of Australia

► Australia covers a continent, but most people live along the coasts and near rivers.

MAP SKILL Use Latitude and Longitude *What city is located at about 10°S, 130°E?*

The large central part of Australia is mostly desert or dry grassland. This region is called the outback. Very few people live here. In summer, daytime temperatures are often more than 100° F. To escape the heat, some people live in underground homes.

The outback is rich in gold and other minerals. Trucks and trains travel hundreds of miles to bring food and supplies to people living in the outback.

Some farmers raise sheep and cattle in the outback. Their ranches are called stations. Some stations are as large as small countries and depend on their own wells and power generators. People might be days away from the nearest neighbor. Most children living on stations study at home. They use two-way radios and computers to "attend" school.

REVIEW What are two reasons why most Australian communities are located on the coastal plains?
Cause and Effect

Literature and Social Studies

Waltzing Matilda

Australian poet A. B. (Banjo) Paterson wrote "Waltzing Matilda" in 1895 after visiting a station in the outback. It became a famous Australian song. Use the vocabulary list to understand what he wrote about in this verse.

Vocabulary List:

swagman   a traveler

billabong   a water hole

coolibah   a tree that grows near water

billy   a can used to boil water for tea

waltzing matilda   traveling with possessions rolled in a blanket

*Once a jolly swagman
  camped by a billabong,
Under the shade of a
  coolibah tree,
And he sang as he watched and
  waited 'til his billy boiled
"Who'll come a-waltzing,
  Matilda, with me?"*

The History of Australia

The first people to live in Australia were the Aborigines. Aborigines traveled and hunted all over the continent thousands of years ago. They did not write their history on paper. Aborigines remembered and told long stories about their history, beliefs, traditions, and accomplishments. This spoken record is called the *Dreamtime.*

In 1770, Captain James Cook of England explored the eastern coast of Australia. He claimed Australia for the king of England. The land had been home to Aborigines for thousands of years. In 1788, the first British settlement was founded on the coast of Australia, where Sydney is today. The new settlers fought with the Aborigines and forced them into the outback.

In 1851, miners discovered gold in the outback. People came from all over the world to search for wealth. The gold rush caused roads and towns to be developed in the outback.

▶ **Many Aboriginal legends tell of the giant rock known as Uluru. Aborigines painted nearby caves with scenes from their history.**

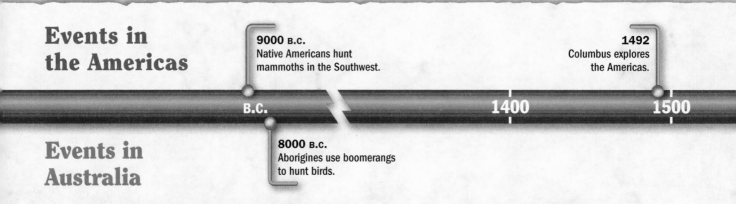

Events in the Americas

9000 B.C.
Native Americans hunt mammoths in the Southwest.

1492
Columbus explores the Americas.

B.C.   1400   1500

Events in Australia

8000 B.C.
Aborigines use boomerangs to hunt birds.

By 1898, Australia needed its own government. Australian leaders wrote a constitution and presented it to the British. In 1901, Australia became a new nation. For many years, Aborigines were not allowed to vote in elections. Australians have now passed laws to protect and respect all cultural traditions.

▶ This painting by J. W. Burtt shows Aboriginal leaders meeting with Englishman John Batman in 1835. The Aborigines signed a treaty giving land to John Batman.

DOCUMENT-BASED QUESTION

How are the people in the painting alike and different?

REVIEW Based on the events shown on the time line, explain how the histories of Australia and the United States are the same. How are they different? **Compare and Contrast**

DOCUMENT-BASED QUESTION

How many years after Jamestown was settled did the British settle Sydney?

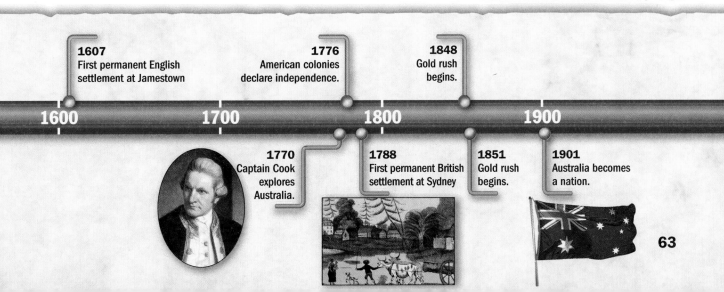

1607
First permanent English settlement at Jamestown

1776
American colonies declare independence.

1848
Gold rush begins.

1600 1700 1800 1900

1770
Captain Cook explores Australia.

1788
First permanent British settlement at Sydney

1851
Gold rush begins.

1901
Australia becomes a nation.

The Government of Australia

Australia is a member of the Commonwealth of Nations. Most nations in this group used to be British colonies. Australia has its own government, constitution, and laws. The prime minister is the head of Australia's government.

Parliament makes Australia's laws and plans its policies. Parliament, like the United States Congress, has a Senate and a House of Representatives. The Australian people elect leaders to represent them in Parliament. After elections, the leader of the party with the most winners in Parliament becomes prime minister.

Australia has six states and two territories. Territories are parts of a country not yet organized as states. Each state and territory elects its own local leaders. Local police and courts enforce the laws and settle disputes.

▶ This rural police officer is working to keep Australian citizens safe.

▶ The Australian government meets in Parliament House. It is in Canberra, the capital of Australia.

Australia is a nation of immigrants. People of many countries and cultures live in Australia. The government develops laws to ensure that all of these groups have the same rules, rights, and responsibilities. Australia's laws give people of every culture the freedom to follow their traditions.

Like Native Americans in the United States, Australia's Aborigines are made up of many different groups. Leaders from these groups are elected to work with the Australian government. These leaders help the government make decisions, solve problems, and plan ways to support the Aborigines and their culture.

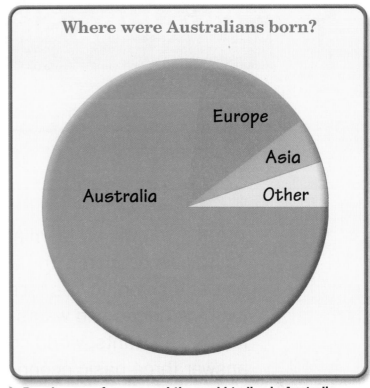

Where were Australians born?

▶ People come from around the world to live in Australia.

🔍 **DOCUMENT-BASED QUESTION** *According to the pie chart, where are most Australians born? What is the largest immigrant group in Australia?*

REVIEW Describe how the government of Australia is organized. **Summarize**

▶ Australian Aborigines perform a traditional dance during opening ceremonies of the 2000 Summer Olympics in Sydney, Australia.

Think About Economic Questions

What? You will be learning more about Australia's economy. You already know that all world communities face the challenge of meeting needs and wants. In order to meet needs and wants, world communities must answer three basic economic questions. Economics is the study of how goods and services are produced and distributed.

Why? Trade, or the buying and selling of goods and services, helps people get the things they need and want.

How? Knowing how to plan an economic trade will help you understand how an economy works.

Kara lives in the city of Adelaide in southern Australia. She wants to earn money during summer vacation. Thinking about the three economic questions on the next page will help Kara plan her trade.

What goods and services should be produced and how much should be produced?
Kara decides to make and sell lemonade. She has lemon trees in her yard, water, and $7.00 to buy sugar and paper cups. She also has a juicer, jug, and a small table. Kara has counted 60 to 80 people passing by her house each day. She can make enough lemonade to serve about 50 of them.

How shall goods and services be produced?
First Kara buys the sugar and paper cups. She picks the lemons from the trees in her yard. Then she squeezes the lemons and mixes the juice with water and sugar in a jug. When she sells one jug of lemonade, she will make another. Now it is time for Kara to set up a table by the sidewalk and make a sign that says "Lemonade 25¢ a Cup."

Think and Apply

1. How could you use these three economic questions to plan a trade?

2. What human resources, capital resources, and natural resources were used to make and sell lemonade?

3. How will Kara know if the lemonade stand was successful?

Who will buy the goods and services?
Kara lives near the beach. People walk down the sidewalk in front of her house to go to the beach. She will sell the lemonade to people walking to and from the beach.

The Economy of Australia

Australia has a strong economy. Trading with other countries is an important part of the economy. When people trade, they buy or sell goods and services. Australia is rich in farm goods and minerals. Trading these resources with other countries creates many jobs in Australia. Almost one in five jobs in Australia is tied somehow to trade.

Some other countries cannot produce the amount of goods and services they need. For example, Australia sells wool, meat, and grain to Japan. In exchange, Australia can get phones and computers from Japan.

▶ Almost three-fourths of the grain, produce, sugar, meat, and milk produced in Australia is traded to other countries. Australia also supplies coal, iron ore, and other minerals, such as this opal, to world communities.

Land Use and Resources in Australia

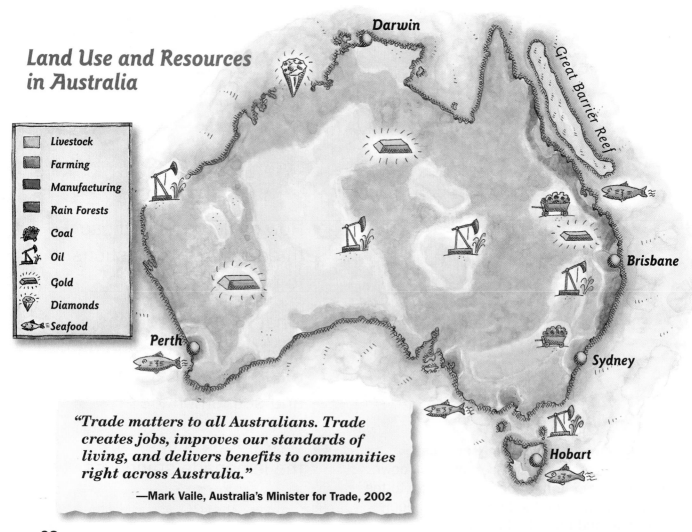

Legend:
- Livestock
- Farming
- Manufacturing
- Rain Forests
- Coal
- Oil
- Gold
- Diamonds
- Seafood

Darwin

Great Barrier Reef

Brisbane

Perth

Sydney

Hobart

"Trade matters to all Australians. Trade creates jobs, improves our standards of living, and delivers benefits to communities right across Australia."

—Mark Vaile, Australia's Minister for Trade, 2002

Australia also sells services. Tourism is an important service in Australia. Stores, restaurants, and hotels provide services for tourists. When tourists visit Australia, the money they spend helps the economy.

Australia has some of the world's rarest animals and environments. These environments and animals are part of Australia's resources. Australia's economic growth depends on its resources. People in Australia must decide how to develop, protect, and make use of its resources. That way, Australia's resources will continue to help its economy grow.

REVIEW Why are natural resources important to Australia's economy?
Cause and Effect

▶ **Many tourists come to visit Australia's Great Barrier Reef, the world's largest coral reef.**

UNIT 5 ◀ REVIEW AND ASSESS

1. What holiday do Australians celebrate on January 26? Why?
2. Compare features of Australia's outback with features of its coastal plains.
3. What effect did the 1788 British settlement of Sydney have on the Aborigines?
4. How does the Australian government support and represent the Aborigines?
5. Write a paragraph telling what factors influence Australia's economic decisions.

Tying It All Together

Based on the time line on pages 62–63, the painting on page 63, and the graph on page 65, how do you know that Australia is a country influenced by different cultures?

Touring Australia

No other country is like Australia! These fun projects will help you learn more about Australia's people, land, and animals. Do these projects in a group or by yourself.

Visit Sunny Australia!

Make a poster. Suppose you own a travel agency in Australia. Research some popular tourist sites in Australia. Look for interesting cities. Find out about environmental areas such as the rain forest and the outback. Make a travel poster for one or more Australian sites. Try to make a poster that would convince tourists to come visit Australia.

Visit the Outback!

AUSTRALIAN	AMERICAN
Arvo	Afternoon
Fair dinkum	Honest, true
Hooly Dooly!	Wow!
Jumbuck	Sheep
Mate	Friend
Milk Bar	Corner store
Oz	Australia
Ta	Thanks

Tales from Down Under

Tell a story. Form a group. Study the list of Australian terms. Take turns telling each other stories using some of these terms. Ask the listeners to name the American words for the Australian terms in each story.

Rock Art

Draw a picture. Long ago many Aborigines created rock carvings and rock paintings inside caves. Find books with pictures of rock art by Aborigines. Study the ways Aborigines from the past drew pictures of animals in their rock art paintings. Draw and color a picture of your favorite animal in the same style.

How Big Is Australia?

Measure distances. Form a group. Find a map of Australia and a map of the United States. Make sure both maps list major cities and have a mileage scale. Measure the distance from Melbourne to Brisbane, Melbourne to Alice Springs, and Melbourne to Perth. Use the scale to find out how many miles are in each distance. Find your home town on the map of the United States. Find three places in the United States that are about the same distance from your town as the ones you measured on the map of Australia.

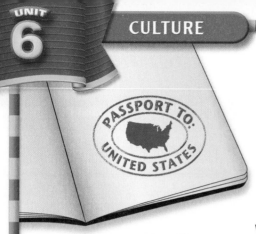

Welcome to the United States!

Hello! My name is Keisha. I live in Washington, D.C. I live with my parents and sisters in an apartment. We enjoy the beautiful parks, government buildings, museums, and theaters in Washington, D.C.

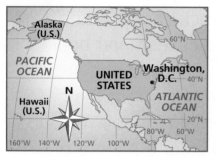

I ride a bus to school. My classmates come from all over the city. My school is partners with the Smithsonian Institution, so on school days we often visit one of the museums. Students get to study museum objects and set up exhibits in the classroom. We like that!

My father works at the United States Mint Headquarters. The United States Mint makes the coins that are used in this country. My mother is a guide at the United States Capitol. Many people in Washington, D.C., have government jobs like my parents do. That is because the city is our nation's capital.

Washington, D.C., has many exciting events. My favorite is the Smithsonian Folklife Festival, which is held every summer. It includes everything from Native American dancing to Japanese cooking.

▶ **Keisha is nine years old. Her family likes to visit the historical sights in Washington, D.C.**

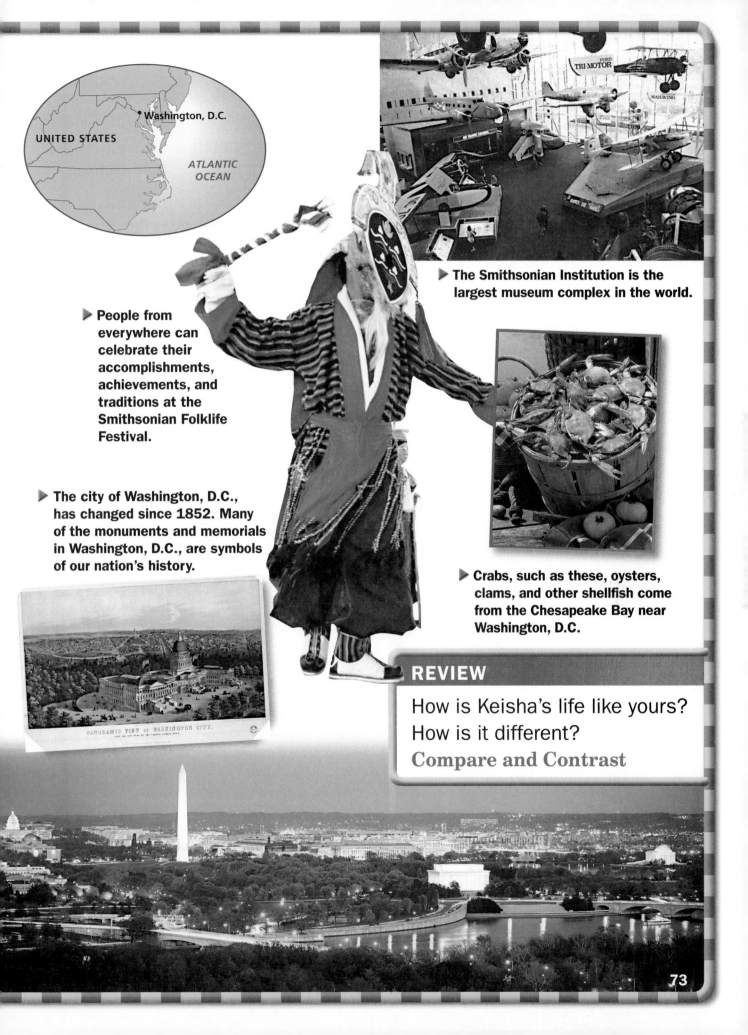

UNITED STATES

• Washington, D.C.

ATLANTIC OCEAN

▶ The Smithsonian Institution is the largest museum complex in the world.

▶ People from everywhere can celebrate their accomplishments, achievements, and traditions at the Smithsonian Folklife Festival.

▶ The city of Washington, D.C., has changed since 1852. Many of the monuments and memorials in Washington, D.C., are symbols of our nation's history.

PANORAMIC VIEW OF WASHINGTON CITY.

▶ Crabs, such as these, oysters, clams, and other shellfish come from the Chesapeake Bay near Washington, D.C.

REVIEW

How is Keisha's life like yours? How is it different?
Compare and Contrast

The Geography of the United States

The United States is located in North America. It is south of Canada and north of Mexico. The United States can be divided into five regions: the West, Southwest, Midwest, Northeast, and Southeast. Each region has its own landforms and climate, or physical environment.

People depend on their physical environments in different ways. Fishermen who live in the Northeast region depend on fish from the Atlantic Ocean to make their living. Farmers in the Midwest region depend on rich farmland to help them produce the crops they sell.

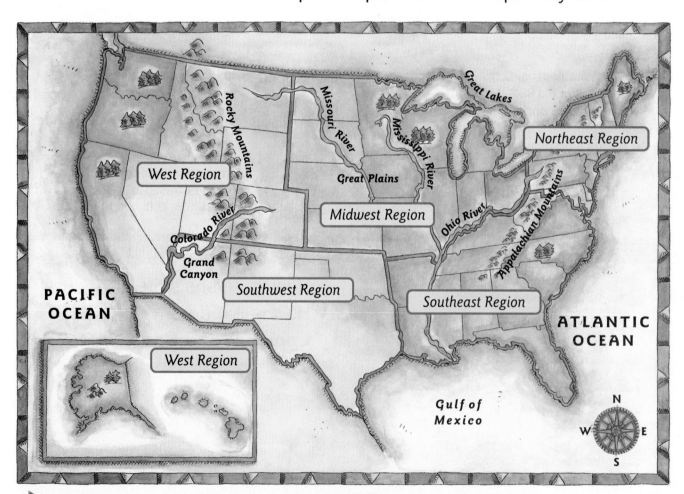

▶ Though they are far away, Alaska and Hawaii are considered part of the West Region.

DOCUMENT-BASED QUESTION *Name some of the special features, such as landforms and bodies of water, that you see on this United States map.*

Geographic factors often determine where people settle. Most major United States cities were built near waterways so goods could be moved easily. Many towns were settled where natural resources, such as ore or coal, were found. Jobs, such as mining, attracted workers to those areas. Some places, like the desert, are very hot and dry, so people wishing to settle there had to figure out a way to get water to these dry places.

▶ This satellite-produced image shows where United States cities and towns are located.

REVIEW Give two examples of how people in different regions of the United States depend on their physical environments.
Main Idea and Details

United States Extremes	
Highest Point	Mt. McKinley in Alaska – 20,320 feet high
Lowest Point	Death Valley in California – 282 feet below sea level
Longest River	Missouri River – 2,540 miles long
Driest Place	Death Valley – less than 2 inches of rain per year
Wettest Place	Mount Waialeale in Hawaii – about 460 inches of rain per year

🔍 **DOCUMENT-BASED QUESTION** Which place gets the most rain per year? Which place gets the least rain per year?

▶ Death Valley

Use a Bar Graph

What? You know the different regions of the United States have different kinds of climates. Temperature is an important part of climate. In some places the temperature can be very high. In other places it can be very low. If you want to compare temperatures of different places, you might use a bar graph. A **bar graph** uses bars to show data. Look at the bar graph below. It compares the average January temperatures of five cities located in different parts of the United States. Each city has its own bar.

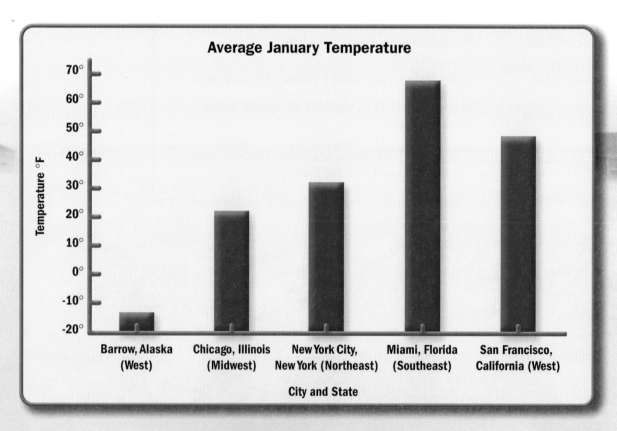

Average January Temperature

Temperature °F — 70° 60° 50° 40° 30° 20° 10° 0° -10° -20°

Barrow, Alaska (West) • Chicago, Illinois (Midwest) • New York City, New York (Northeast) • Miami, Florida (Southeast) • San Francisco, California (West)

City and State

Why? A bar graph can help you compare an amount or number. It shows you at a glance how things relate to one another.

How? When you read a bar graph, look at the graph title. It tells you what information the graph shows. Look at the words and numbers along the left side and bottom. They tell you what is being measured and where it is being measured. Each bar on the graph shows the average January temperature of a selected city. You can see which city is the coldest that month and which is the warmest.

1. Which city has the lowest average January temperature?

2. Which city has an average January temperature of about 49°F?

3. On average, about how many degrees warmer is Miami, Florida, than New York City, New York, in January?

The History of the United States

The United States is a blend of people, ideas, and cultures from all over the world. Native Americans have lived on this land for thousands of years. Then explorers from Spain, England, and France arrived on the shores of North America. English colonists came in the 1600s looking for a better life. Some hoped to get rich. Others were looking for religious freedom. Life for the early colonists was hard. People cleared land for farms. Towns and cities grew up in the colonies. People from other parts of Europe arrived in the Americas.

Many of the colonists wanted their independence from England. In 1776 colonial leaders wrote and signed the Declaration of Independence. Colonists had to fight England to be free. After winning the war, the 13 colonies became the United States of America.

The United States has grown and changed over the past 200 years. More people have come to this country. Together Americans have faced both hard times and times of good fortune.

Literature and Social Studies

The United States is made up of many cultures and ethnic groups. An eighth-grader in Los Angeles wrote this poem about how she feels to be an American. Do you agree with her ideas?

....

How can you label me?
My mother's from Guatemala,
My father's from Honduras,
My grandmother's from Belize,
My grandfather's from Jamaica.
And it goes back so much
*   further.*
I speak English and Spanish.
So do you label me Hispanic?
Or Black-Hispanic?
Or "Blaxican"?
Here's an idea:
Don't label me at all.

—From *Los Angeles Times*, February 5, 1999.

🔍 **DOCUMENT-BASED QUESTION**

How would you describe the writer's family history?

The Civil War was fought between the northern states and the southern states from 1861 to 1865. This war divided our nation, but it helped put an end to slavery.

As the Civil War ended, the United States became more industrialized. Then during the Great Depression in the 1930s, many people lost their jobs. Thousands of stores, banks, and even schools had to close. But the nation recovered. The government put many people to work by creating jobs, such as building bridges, dams, and housing developments. Writers were paid to record oral histories, or people's experiences told in their own words.

With great courage, the United States has faced wars and terrorism. Today it remains a strong and unified country.

REVIEW Name some hard times that Americans have faced in our country's history. **Main Idea and Details**

"Our individual stomachs were full . . . we were congenial [friendly] souls, and as men at peace and who neither regret 'yesterday' nor fear 'tomorrow,' we were in the mood for talk."

—Library of Congress
WPA Federal Writers' Project Collection

▶ During the Great Depression, many people told oral histories about their lives. Oral histories are just one way people can learn about the values, ideas, beliefs, and traditions of others.

▶ During the Great Depression, people without jobs stood in long lines to get food.

▶ **United States citizens go to voting places to elect government leaders. Citizens must be at least 18 years old to vote.**

▶ **The state capitol in Albany, New York, is one of only a few state capitols without a dome roof.**

The Government of the United States

The United States has three branches of government: the executive, the legislative, and the judicial. The President heads the executive branch. This branch enforces laws and directs the armed forces. The legislative branch is made up of the Congress. This branch makes laws and sets taxes. The third branch is the judicial branch, or courts. This branch decides what laws mean and if laws follow the Constitution. Laws help groups of people live together, because everyone has the same rules to follow.

Each of the fifty states also has leaders who make rules and laws. Each state has a governor, legislators, and judges. A governor is the leader of a state's executive branch. Legislators make state laws. Judges interpret, or decide, what laws mean.

FACT FILE

The Supreme Court

The Supreme Court is the highest court of the land. Supreme Court judges are appointed by the President, but they must be approved by one part of Congress, the Senate. There are nine justices on the Supreme Court.

The Supreme Court building is an important landmark. The words "Equal Justice Under Law" are shown on the front of the building. The doors are made of bronze, and they are very heavy. Each door weighs 13,000 pounds!

People are welcome to sit in on court sessions. They can also tour the building. Many people visit the Supreme Court each year.

▶ The Supreme Court building was built in 1935.

Sometimes people have conflicts over rules, rights, and responsibilities. These conflicts are settled in different ways in different countries. One way to settle these conflicts in the United States is in court. There judges listen to both sides of the problem. They decide how the problem should be settled.

REVIEW Identify the three branches of the United States government and explain the role of each branch. **Main Idea and Details**

The Economy of the United States

The United States produces more goods and services than any other country in the world. The United States also has many natural resources, such as coal for fuel, timber for paper, and rich farmland.

The abundance of natural resources, important to economic growth, means that the United States does not have to depend as much on other countries for resources. Still, people and businesses in the United States must make hard decisions. How much and what kinds of goods and services should they buy from other countries? How much should they sell?

▶ Oil is an important natural resource. Most oil is used as a fuel.

Food for Many Nations

Then and Now In the early years of the United States, most people worked on farms. But as time went by, things changed. New equipment and ways of farming meant fewer people were needed for farm work. People began moving to cities in search of jobs. Today fewer than 2 million of the more than 280 million people in the United States are farmers. But farmers still have an important job. American farmers provide food not only for this country but also for people all over the world. The United States is sometimes called the "breadbasket of the world."

▶ Wheat harvest 1870

▶ Wheat harvest today

The United States economy also depends on human resources. Some people own businesses, such as stores and restaurants. Other people work in factories where they make products such as cars and computers. Some people work in service industries such as banking and health care. Service workers have jobs helping others.

You have read about the Great Depression. That was a difficult economic time. But today the United States economy is much stronger.

REVIEW What decisions do people and businesses in the United States have to make about the economy?
Main Idea and Details

▶ Health care is an important service in the United States economy.

UNIT 6 ◀ REVIEW AND ASSESS

Check Facts and Main Ideas

1. What kind of jobs are found in Washington, D.C.? Why?
2. Give examples of how geographic features determine where people settle.
3. Explain some events that have changed the United States since the 1700s.
4. How does the United States government make and enforce laws?
5. Make a word web showing either the natural resources or the human resources that make the economy of the United States strong.

Tying It All Together

Based on the map on page 74, the chart on page 75, and the poem on page 78, what kinds of diversity, or differences, make up the United States? Write one or more paragraphs to answer this question.

Touring North America

The United States is only one of the countries in North America. Now learn more about all of North America. Here are fun projects to do alone or in a group.

An Exciting Vacation

Make a poster. Choose a place in North America you would like to visit. Find out about it. Look for any monuments or memorials located there. Make a travel poster advertising the place you researched. Display your poster in the classroom.

Learn About Traders

Make a diorama. Research the fur trade in Canada during the 1700s and 1800s. Look for historical narratives told by people who lived during this time. Give an oral report to your class about what you learned. Make a diorama to go with your report.

Pack Your Bags

Play a game. In a group, research the climate of a vacation spot in North America. Discuss the things you would take on a trip there. Then play a game. Have a group member say "I am going on a trip to ____ and I am taking a ____." Have the next person repeat what was said and add another item. Continue until only one player can repeat all the items that have been named.

Ancient Ruins!

Research life of long ago. Read about the Aztec or Mayan cultures of Mexico. Suppose you could interview a member of that culture. Write an account of the oral history that person might tell you. Make a model or sculpture to go with your report.

Index

Titles appear in italics. Page numbers after an *m* refer to a map. Page numbers after a *p* refer to a photograph. Page numbers after a *c* refer to a chart or graph. The terms *See* and *See also* direct the reader to alternative entries.

Credits